Lilies

Cover photograph
A fine group of *Lilium regale*.
Photograph by Valerie Finnis.

Overleaf
Lilium 'Iona', a hybrid raised by Dr Chris North at the Scottish Crop Research Institute (see p.48).
Photograph by Martyn Symmons

Cassell Educational Limited
Artillery House
Artillery Row
London SW1P 1RT
for the Royal Horticultural Society

First Published 1985
Second impression 1987

British Library Cataloguing in Publication Data

Fox, Derek
  Lilies.
  1. Lilies
  I. Title   II. Royal Horticultural Society
  635.9′34324   SB413.L7

ISBN 0-304-31117-0

Line drawings by Sue Wickison
based on those in *Growing Lilies* by Derek Fox (Croom Helm 1985) and reproduced by kind permission of the publishers.
Photographs by Pat Brindley, Duncan Coombs, Valerie Finnis, Derek Fox, Polly Lyster, National Seed Development Organisation Ltd., Martyn Rix and Martyn Simmons

Design by Lynda Smith

Phototypesetting by Georgia Origination Ltd, Formby
Printed in Hong Kong by Wing King Tong Co. Ltd

CONTENTS

'Limelight' a hybrid with trumpet-shaped flowers.

Introduction

If the rose is the symbol of kings and queens, the lily is the flower of the gods. Gods in their heavens are much inclined to be temperamental, and the lily has often been considered a similar plant in cultivation. However, the following pages are written to show that the lily can be brought down to earth and when treated in accordance with its particular, but in no way difficult, needs, can grace our gardens and give us joy like no other flower. The commoner lilies grown today are not, and must not be considered, difficult to grow. Of the many excellent hybrids available none has the reputation of being a problem child for if that were so they would not be available commercially. What is very important is that bulbs should be purchased only if in tip-top condition otherwise they should be spurned, like overripe strawberries.

'Anne Boleyn', an upright-facing hybrid.

What is a lily?

The lily is one of the most renowned flowers in the garden, yet it is not very well known and is much confused with other plants which have willingly linked themselves to the name of lily (see p.22).

The lily is a bulbous herbaceous perennial. It is a monocotyledon, in the genus *Lilium* in the family Liliaceae closely allied to amaryllids and irises and even orchids, and not so far removed from grasses and sedges.

The flowers, whether singly, a few, or many on a stem, come in various forms, though they are all basically similar. A typical flower, like *L. speciosum* (see below) displays the parts very well.

Parts of the lily flower.

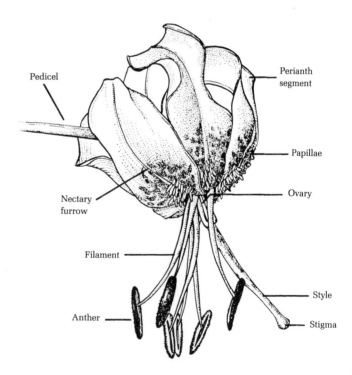

There are six 'petals'. More precisely there are three outer sepals, being those which are seen when the flower is in bud, and three inner petals. They are usually similarly coloured and are attached to the stem behind the ovary. The petals have nectary furrows towards their bases, which exude sweet nectar, and sometimes have papillae–knobbly excrescences–to a lesser or greater extent on either side. Spotting on the inner surface of the petals is common, but not on all lilies, varying from a slight amount near the base to an excessive covering to the tips.

A thin style ending in a trilobed stigma is attached to the ovary and this is surrounded by six filaments to which at the tip of each is attached an anther often swinging freely when bearing the sticky heavy pollen.

Flowers are positioned in differing ways. Possibly the commonest seen, though rarely the most elegant, face upright (see below) and being generally much shorter than ourselves appear dominant in colour rather than form. They are sometimes referred to as crocus-shaped, but this is more for convenience rather than exactness of description. The petals recurve slightly and usually only at the tips.

'Connecticut King', a bright yellow Asiatic hybrid (see p.48)

Opposite: 'Red Lion', an example of an upright-facing lily.
Above: 'Cover Girl', a hybrid of *L. auratum* × *L. speciosum*.
Below: *Lilium candidum* grows well in a mixed border (see also p.33).

Outward facing flowers (see p.11) may be very similar to the up-right kinds, especially if they belong to one of the vast range of Asiatic hybrids. However these flowers rarely occur in nature. They may be more recurved than upright flowers. Otherwise, both in the wild and in our gardens, the commonest outward facing lilies are trumpet-shaped particularly exemplified by L. *regale* (see cover) and the many yellow and pink coloured hybrids seen today. Mention must also be made of the Madonna lily, L. *candidum* (see p.33) although it is in a different class, which has a shorter bell. These lilies have elegance and often beautiful poise and are frequently as notable for the colour of the outside of the petal as the inner. In the many hybrids the degree of recurving of the petals greatly affects the character of the flower.

The pendent lilies owe as much to the pedicels or flower stalks as to the flowers themselves for their grace and charm. Typical of these kinds are the turkscap flowers, like the tightly-rolled petals of the numerous-flowered martagon lilies (see opposite). How-ever, these in their best forms are with their short flower stalks no match for the best of the *lankongense* × *davidii* hybrids produced by Dr North or the generally taller hybrids of western American species. The latter often have much elegance and airy beauty with the less-recurved petals.

Lilium pomponium, a fine example of a turkscap flower.

Lilium martagon (see p.43), sometimes found naturalised in Britain.

Above: A pendent-flowered Asiatic hybrid (see p.46).
Below: A Yeates × *parkmanii* hybrid group.

Lilium szovitsianum, the Caucasian Lily (see p.46).

Lilium auratum (see p.52), a species originating from Japan.

Some of the other flower shapes are less easy to define or categorise. There is the recurved flower of L. *speciosum* (see p.8) like the equally well-known L. *henryi*, which basically is a turkscap, but surely with a difference. There is the other main partner in the Oriental hybrids, L. *auratum*, which may be referred to as bowl-shaped (see above), but here the very large size is, perhaps, the most important feature. In the hybrids, more commonly grown today, there is every gradation of flower shape between the two species. Further there are now many hybrids

incorporating Japanese trumpet-shaped species, which give yet
another range of shape. Caucasian lilies, like L. *szovitsianum* (see
p.15), are in another group not too easily defined. They vary in
angle of disposition from horizontal to pendent and have less
sharply recurved petals, sometimes being described as funnel–
campanulate. Last to be described here, but by no means the least
is the inflorescence of L. *canadense* (see below). Thought by many
to be most beautiful, there is the curving line of the pedicel
followed by the elegance of the finest campanulate form in the
flower.

Lilium canadense, a species from North America.

Flower colour in lilies may be likened to those other great groups of garden plants, rhododendrons, roses and chrysanthemums, but to which they bear no relation. None of them has any true blues, and fortunately no lily has tried to mimic blue. Besides white, the most commonly seen lilies are within the yellow–orange–fiery red spectrum of which the yellows and the deeper reds are the most acceptable. However there are pinks in many shades which are aesthetically very pleasing. The richer and deeper shades, which may be described as crimsons, are superb while fresh, but die rather sadly. The paler shades of pink may therefore be considered more enjoyable even through to the latter stages of life than the bolder tones. Spotting, usually dark and frequently a deep maroon, or lack of spotting, is a most important attention-seeking device. Gross overspotting as it may be termed is rarely seen in the more commonly grown lilies, but spotless varieties are common today especially amongst the Asiatics. They exhibit a brilliance over a broad flower area, which, to the more sensitive, can be overpowering. Gorgeous though they are, like 'Marilyn Monroe' (see p.47), care should be taken in their selection and placing.

Before leaving the flower it should be noted that the vital sexual parts, the anthers with their pollen sacs and the viscose stigma, are both very prominent to the human eye. This makes it easy to effect pollination and, if the circumstances are right, produce a new batch of the species, new varieties or new hybrids.

Stems may be taken for granted, but no lily performs properly without one. They carry the inflorescence and the leaves and if the stem is broken off, has its head eaten out on emergence or, at a later stage, is eaten through by a slug, then that is all the gardener will see of it for the year. Generally the bulb will be weakened by the lack of performance, so accidents and the actions of predators must be kept to a minimum.

Leaves are another vital organ and in most kinds are fairly prolifically displayed up the stem. They add greatly to the look and balance of the plant. They are simple and entire, often scattered or spirally arranged, but sometimes, as in the martagons and many American species, the leaves are in whorls (verticillate) with a few scattered at top and bottom. It behoves every lily grower to try to keep the leaves of his plants clean and healthy.

When thinking of a bulb we usually imagine something like an onion–something edible! Although the lily bulb is edible–to more than one animal species might it be said–it is not composed of concentric rings of tissue enclosed in a protective sheath, but comprises a basal plate on which are formed a number of scales. Generally these are tight and compact, but the whole is usually

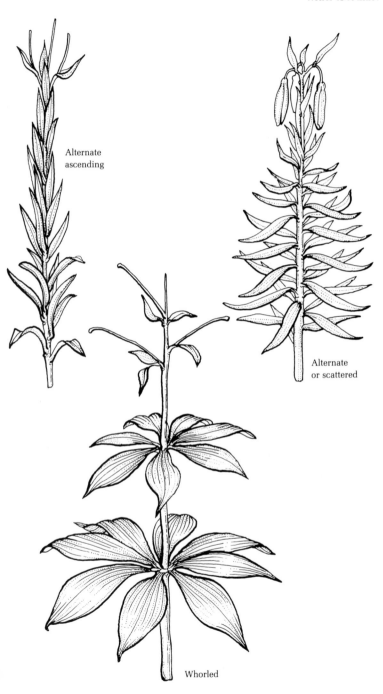

Alternate
ascending

Alternate
or scattered

Whorled

Some of the different arrangements of leaves.

much more vulnerable to damage than the onion. Most cultivated lilies have concentric bulbs (see below) where the scales, sometimes waisted or jointed, are variable in width, but normally tightly imbricated. Many North American lilies have what appear to be quite different bulbs. Most of those from the eastern side are

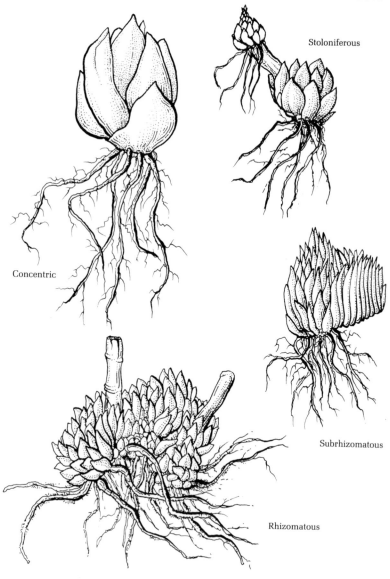

Above and opposite: Different types of lily bulbs.

said to be stoloniferous (see opposite), that is, in producing their new bulb for the coming season they send out a thick horizontal shoot from the current bulb at the end of which a new basically concentric bulb forms. Many of the western American lily bulbs are described as rhizomatous or subrhizomatous (see opposite). The latter gradually elongate in one direction, while the former stretch out a limb every year, but, unlike the roundish stolon with a scattering of scales of the eastern kind, it is a flat basal plate covered with a mass of small usually jointed scales. The more vigorous kinds may grow more than one branch per year and effectively build up a whole mass of bulb tissue.

Some lilies are said to be stoloniform (see below). Although implied it really has nothing to do with the bulb. What happens is that from a concentric bulb the growing stem wanders underground for some inches before emerging. It will emit roots into the soil and in season produce a few young bulblets so lilies are often referred to as stem-rooting or not stem-rooting. Those that are, and it includes most Asiatic hybrids, trumpet lilies, the Oriental hybrids and martagons, welcome deep planting where conditions are suitable, or mulching, and enjoy the benefit they can obtain from a rich humus layer of top soil as long as it can be kept reasonably moist at least through the main growing season. Confined to a few species this growth is still witnessed to a lesser extent in some hybrids. It is not uncommon for vertical stems below ground to issue root growth or produce bulblets. This point will be mentioned again under cultivation and propagation.

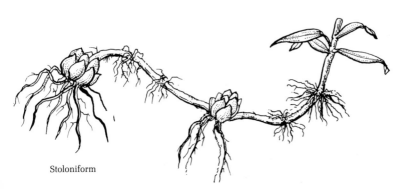

Stoloniform

What is considered by very many to be one of the more important attributes of lilies is the scent. As with roses this is plentiful in some, absent in others. In a few it is universally accepted as close to repellent, but in many kinds it is irreverently consuming and exciting. The truth is, though, that the vast majority of lilies grown are the Asiatic hybrids and they have little or no perfume. The gardener who wants scent must choose the right lilies such as the Oriental hybrids and many of the trumpet lilies. Scent comes from L. martagon and Caucasian lilies, but it may not be appreciated by all.

It is right to mention cardiocrinums here. To gardeners they are different, but still lilies. It takes many years to grow a bulb to maturity, but when that occurs it produces a fine strong, often tall, stem clothed in broad rich green leaves terminated by many lovely white wine-washed trumpet flowers (see opposite). From this it sets seeds and the bulb expires leaving behind a few bulblets. Cardiocrinum giganteum and its variety yunnanense are native to monsoon-soaked forests of the Himalayas and further east, but are not difficult to grow in woodland conditions in this country.

Referring back to the beginning the following are some of the plants that have taken the name of lily:

African Corn Lily	=	Ixia
African Lily	=	Agapanthus
Arum Lily	=	Zantedeschia
Belladona Lily	=	Amaryllis belladonna
Bluebead Lily	=	Clintonia borealis
Bugle Lily	=	Watsonia
Day Lily	=	Hemerocallis
Glory Lily	=	Gloriosa
Guernsey Lily	=	Nerine sarniensis
Kaffir Lily	=	Schizostylis
Lily of the Valley	=	Convallaria
Lily Pink	=	Aphyllanthes
Peruvian Lily	=	Alstroemeria
Plantain Lily	=	Hosta
St Bernard's Lily	=	Anthericum liliago
St Bruno's Lily	=	Paradisea liliastrum
Scarborough Lily	=	Vallota speciosa
Toad Lily	=	Tricyrtis
Torch Lily	=	Kniphofia
Trout Lily	=	Erythronium
Voodoo Lily	=	Sauromatum guttatum
Water Lily	=	Nuphar and Nymphaea
Wood Lily (other than Lilium philadelphicum)	=	Trillium

Cardiocrinum giganteum at Inverewe on the west coast of Scotland.

Where to grow lilies

In view of the fact that there are approximately one hundred species of lily in the wild covering a vast area in the northern hemisphere mainly in the temperate zone, it is not difficult to imagine that there must be some lilies which could prove suitable to any garden we care to name. The making of hybrids has given us more tractable lilies and this makes the situation even easier.

It is recognised that the climate of Britain is moderate enough to grow a vast range of the world's plants outdoors and so it is found that the great majority of lilies are considered hardy throughout Britain without protection. This is not to say they are all well suited across the country; nor is it suggested that as gardeners we have the whole land at our spade. Few of us have more than our own little patch and we find the problems that creates are enough.

Where our climate may let us down is in its unevenness or its lack of adherence to fairly rigid seasonal patterns. Spring can often prove the most difficult period of the year and those who happen to garden in a frost pocket may easily find their young lilies cut or damaged by frost in some years. This, of course, does not solely apply to lilies, but to many plants. Another factor is rain. On the eastern side of the country the rainfall may often prove too little at the time it is required and welcomed by lilies. On the western side the rainfall will generally be quite adequate, but the atmosphere may often prove too moist especially as summer progresses, and damage and disease to the foliage and flowers may result. These are of necessity generalisations and every gardener must learn to judge the microclimate of his own beds and borders. Watering may, despite what is said about good drainage later on, often prove necessary, but kept as far as possible at ground level and off the foliage.

What of the soil? Most lilies enjoy a stony, gritty or sandy fast draining compost often with a high humus content. Lilies have long left the alluvial plains if they were ever on them, and been forced into the hills, where they might even be at the streamside, but rarely or never on the flat. Few of us have anything approaching these conditions, but fortunately most of the lilies we might obtain will take to heavier soil conditions. Especially is this so if it can be ensured that soil moisture at all seasons (when not frozen) can seep away from the bulbs and their basal roots. Heavier soils may even have advantages. Firstly they will generally contain a more adequate supply of nutrients, especially the trace elements, and secondly, they will rarely dry out so thoroughly that drought will begin to desiccate the bulb. It is just as likely for an extremely dry condition to weaken a bulb as a wet one. Although most lilies seem to prefer a neutral or not-too-acid soil (pH 5.5–7.0) there are plenty of lilies that are lime tolerant; some even tend to prefer an alkaline soil.

Every garden has many situations and lilies may be found that can fit into most of them. Generally an open site is preferable, but this does not mean an exposed position. The first allows a good many hours of sunshine during the summer when it shines, but not the force of too much wind. Lilies will like the company of other plants, generally of a lower stature, which may help to shade the roots and lower stem and add a bit of extra shelter.

Many lilies will accept a light canopy around and overhead and enjoy the conditions of the woodland garden with an occasional mulch of clean leaf soil and fresh leaf litter, the protection of shrubs to the side and dappled shade from above. 'Leaf soil' I

L. speciosum rubrum growing in light shade.

think of as much finer and further decayed than 'leaf mould', and in fact a dark brown or black matter otherwise indistinguishable from soil but really composed almost entirely of humus. If this is too fine a point then it becomes synonymous with 'leaf mould'. From this it may be seen that the wild garden will be suitable for some of these, especially the various martagons and their hybrids. However the shade must not become too dense nor the competition from other plants too strong, for then the lilies will go into decline; a sort of hibernation, and perform only weakly if at all.

Some people so love their lilies that they wish to have them close at hand and perhaps shown off to the full, so they grow them in pots and tubs and have them placed strategically on the patio or along the terrace. This is an excellent method much to be commended, but it requires more initial work in preparation and the plants need fairly constant attention during the growing and flowering seasons. One of the best ways is to start the bulbs into growth in smaller pots in the greenhouse or in deep frames. At a suitable time when conditions are favourable and spring flowers are over the lilies may be transferred to their summer homes. After all large tubs or urns are rarely suitable for moving about and it is easier to move the lilies. Other small specimens, such as fuchsias, pelargoniums or the gardener's particular fancy, may be added at the same time to continue flowering after the lilies.

Although the vast majority of lilies are considered hardy in the British Isles a few are not so or may be grown nearer to perfection in a greenhouse. *Lilium longiflorum* is one of the tender species so well-known (and commonly referred to as 'Harrisii') in the florist's trade. This lily may, of course, be grown at most seasons if heat is available. Another, *L. speciosum*, with its many varieties although hardy may because of its late flowering (September and sometimes into October) be better grown under glass in colder parts of the country or where frosts tend to come early. These and others easily obtainable allow us to foster our interest in lilies over a much longer period of the year if we have the benefit of a green-house even if unheated. Frost damage if severe will be obvious to any gardener but when moderate it may be difficult to distinguish from a disease like botrytis. Usually the damage is seen along the length of the leaves where the softer tissues between the veins are killed. There is often a chlorotic look to the plant. It would seem that the softest fastest growing parts of lilies prove the most susceptible. If this is near the base of leaves then they will hang

Opposite: *L. martagon album* (see p.43).

limply and soon show the damage of pale brown tissue. Where plants are damaged by any cause they do become more prone to fungal diseases thereafter. Botrytis seems not to be interveinal but attacks all tissues similarly across the leaf.

Coming outdoors again we may repeat that places have been found for lilies in open beds and borders, under light shade, in the woodland and wild garden, and in acid, neutral or alkaline soils. It may be added that several kinds will fit easily into the rock garden, though discretion will need to be used in the exact choice as dwarf stature is not everything. The well-made rock garden in its usually small compass contains many differing sites, possibly each suitable to a particular lily. Lilies may be found for drier situations and, where drainage is good, the wetter parts of the garden. As some take to sun and others accept shade it is obvious that most of the various aspects found around and about the house and garden may be used for lilies.

How to grow lilies

BUYING BULBS

Some aspects of cultivation have been briefly stated in the previous chapter, but there our viewpoint was from the garden, here we start with the bulbs; or better still before obtaining the bulbs. As fewer lilies are grown than many other bulbs and are relatively expensive, they are not so easy to come by. The lily is best planted in the autumn so that with new root growth it may establish itself while the soil temperature is still relatively high, but this does not suit large growers overseas and their importers. For this reason it is usual for our bulbs to arrive too late in the depth of winter. We must then make the best of a bad job. Fortunately there are now a few specialist suppliers of lily bulbs in Britain and these firms should be able to deliver the bulbs in good time for planting before winter, provided, of course, they are ordered early enough. Recently some of the packaged lily bulbs have been coming earlier into the garden centre or supermarket. It is then up to the gardener to buy what he wants at the first opportunity and not leave them to deteriorate on the shelves. This will be good for the lilies, the garden and gardener and please the retailer who may then order greater variety the following season. It cannot be too greatly emphasised that season after season poor flabby dried-up bulbs are offered to unsuspecting gardeners (even by reputable suppliers). Such lilies too long out of the ground will never make viable plants again. However great the enthusiasm and desire to grow lilies it will not overcome the decrepitude of these impoverished things and they must be shunned. Too often lilies are offered as good for spring planting, which is alright if the bulbs are recently lifted from the ground, or been kept in exacting conditions in store. Frequently they have not and have been out of the ground since the previous September and as such must be in poor health. It is definitely a case of let the buyer beware.

SOIL PREPARATION

Having got the bulbs, what is one to do with them? If they are clean and free of any damage, mould or rot and the scales firm, then planting may start. If not, pluck off any withered, badly damaged or diseased scales. A sharp clean knife may be used to remove small pieces of seemingly bad tissue or to remove dead roots, but the blade should be sterilised between use on separate bulbs. If the gardener is keen to ensure his bulbs' continued survival, as a 'belt and braces' operation he may remove a couple of good clean scales from the base and set them aside for propagation (see p.34).

Bulbs being clean but otherwise a little flabby, not too firm, should be placed in a mixture of damp peat and sand, in proportions of about 7 parts to 3 parts. If kept in cool conditions, after two or three weeks they should have plumped up and the first signs of new root growth from the base might be showing. When this has happened potting up or planting out may be begun according to season. If neither operation is practical then the bulbs may be left in their peat–sand mix for a few more weeks as long as they are held in a temperature close to freezing. This is to keep any growth to the minimum. It is surprising how much growth some young bulbs will make even in a domestic refrigerator.

Potting up lily bulbs may be done for a variety of reasons as suggested elsewhere. Should it be temporary, the grower may judge how much care should be given to detail, but if it is to last the whole growing season and, perhaps, a little while beyond then too much care is not possible. Containers may be of plastic or clay, but for mature bulbs they should be as deep as obtainable. 'Long toms' have often been advocated. Whatever pot is used drainage must be very good not only at the start, but more important must stay that way until repotting is needed. A generous layer of washed granite chippings may be put at the bottom of each plastic pot and a compost used containing some loam (preferably sterilised) and plenty of coarse sand and more granite chippings. So a compost based on the John Innes formula with extra sand and grit to make an open mixture should be satisfactory. The aim should be to be able to water the pot thoroughly and frequently without it becoming waterlogged. For clay pots granite chippings may be placed over the usual sherds and a slightly firmer compost used, but the same principles apply regarding watering. However, such must only apply if there is an adequate good water supply and someone to do the job as required. It is no good having pots of lilies drying out during the day for the roots will soon be damaged and killed in the height of summer. As much future trouble may arise to bulbs in over-dry conditions as over-wet.

Outdoor garden cultivation follows normal practice with particular concern given to one or two aspects, notably good drainage. Deeply dug well worked soil should be as free of pests as possible. No lilies should be planted in soil known to contain underground slugs, millipedes and other pests such as leather-jacket and cutworm larvae. Proprietary soil pest killers may be used to clean the soil, but planting should be delayed for a whole season if necessary.

Although never advocated years ago healthy lilies enjoy feeding–the unhealthy cannot use it. Moderate applications before planting of a general fertilizer, well mixed in the soil are beneficial. No large nitrogen content is required so for cheapness Growmore could be used, but John Innes base fertilizer, as used in the compost, with its hoof and horn providing the nitrogen over a longer period would be more satisfactory. Potash is good for building up quality bulbs and dressings of wood ash as available are useful especially if containing broken pieces of charcoal to improve the soil structure. When the ash is very fine it should be seen not to cake the soil surface.

If there are doubts about soil drainage it must be improved before any planting is contemplated. Where the land is sloping or the beds are sufficiently raised, appreciating how deep the bulbs will be placed, any problems should be taken care of naturally. On level surfaces the situation is more difficult. Normally it is no use digging the planting site more deeply, because water is more likely to drain into it than to drain away. It thereby becomes a sump, the opposite of what is required. Answers may be found in building up the bed by a couple of inches, or providing proper land drainage by piping, broken brick or coarse gravel, and making the sump elsewhere close by. A combination of the two suggestions may in practice be the most satisfactory. In providing a raised bed thought must be given to the incidence of local rainfall and the need for the lilies to be watered. Sloping ground often means that spring and summer rains run off the dry surface, so it is better to provide what are in effect small terraces. Here rain is used to the full and artificial watering not wasted.

Heavy loam is no impediment to growing lilies where the drainage is good. However soil structure can be improved by the addition of rock grits (preferably of an acidic nature unless the soil itself has a low pH) and washed coarse sand. Most lilies enjoy plentiful humus in the soil and as a top layer. This may be added in the form of woodland leaf soil, leaf-mould, garden compost, moss or sedge peat. The latter two will be virtually sterile, but care should be taken when adding any of the others to see they are clean samples, not harbouring injurious pests. Again the peats will be acidic in reaction while the leaf soil and compost would have a pH related to their source. Much may be done in the course of time to change the nature of the soil to the benefit of the lilies. Lilies not lime tolerant include the Oriental hybrids having species such as L. *auratum* and L. *speciosum* in their parentage. L. *tigrinum* too is a lime hater and dwindles in alkaline soils. Fortunately most of the Asiatic hybrids, possible due to their mixed blood, are little if at all affected by limey soils. L. *candidum* and L. *testaceum* are better for being on neutral or alkaline soils and this seems to be the case for L. *henryi*. Trumpet lily hybrids are lime tolerant.

PLANTING

Actual planting is now a simple operation. The drainage is now good, the soil structure improved, the fertilizer added, the bulbs clean and plump, the season and temperature suitable for growth, if only slight. A section of the prepared bed is dug out to a depth of 4 to 6 inches (10–15cm) sufficient to contain bulb or bulbs. A handful of coarse sand may be placed where each bulb is to go, allowing 6 inches between bulbs (15cm), allowing more or less room for large or small bulbs respectively. Place the bulb on the sand dibbling any good roots into the sand. Some people lay the bulbs on their sides to help drainage off the bulb. This may be advantageous; it certainly does not upset the bulb's growth. Carefully mark and label the site or area planted and replace the soil over the bulbs. If the lilies are know to be stem-rooting then the addition of more peat or leaf soil into this top soil will be beneficial. Should the top soil be particularly deep then many lilies might enjoy being planted below 6 inches (15cm). The gardener may do this, but most depth seeking lilies have the ability to pull themselves down with their contractile roots. A few lilies are shallowly planted, one of these being the common Madonna lily, L. *candidum* (opposite). This should be planted, preferably in calcareous soil, during its short dormant period in August before making its flush of autumn leaves. A covering of about $\frac{1}{2}$inch of soil (1–2cm) is all that is required for this non–stem rooter. Its hybrid, L. × *testaceum*, will take to lower planting, say up to twice its own bulb height. The majestic and stately cardio-crinums also require shallow planting. These lilies, as they were once called, enjoy woodland and deep woodland humus-rich soils, but like to have their noses hardly covered by the most recent leaf fall. So the soil should be enriched with humus as much as possible and the bulbs planted into the very top layer.

After–care is simple. Lilies must be kept free of slugs at all times, but especially is it necessary to be watchful when the stems are emerging. They can ruin a young stem overnight and then all is lost for another year, because the bulb cannot replace that stem in the same season. Should there be any doubt about water

Detail of the madonna lily, *L. candidum* (see opposite).

shortage in a dry spring, plenty of water may be given at ground level. Preferably it should be kept off the foliage. Later in the season lilies will want to complete their annual life cycle below ground before winter, and so to provide sufficient moisture in the soil after a hot dry summer some watering may again be necessary in the autumn. If the soil is fairly fertile, not too lean and sandy then no more fertilizer is required at least until the following spring. When the ground is mulched or top dressed in winter (beware of bringing in pests) even this may be dispensed with. The ground should be kept free of weeds. Some ground-cover plants look very attractive under lilies and vice versa, but they must not have a too thick and smothering habit, nor must they encourage or harbour pests.

33

Most lilies are substantial and their stems will carry the flowers well, but those that are tall, drawn up by close planting or shade or in an exposed position should be staked in good time. There is no need for anything elaborate or incongruous. Slender bamboo canes seem to be the best choice, not only aesthetically, but for strength and flexibility. Great care should be taken to see that no bulbs are damaged by the canes, remembering that all stems do not emerge immediately above the bulbs. If it is realised beforehand that staking will be required, little sticks may be placed between the bulbs at planting time to mark positions for tall canes later.

During the growing season a watch should be kept for signs of aphids, other pests, botrytis and any troubles on the foliage. Where careful diagnosis suggests a cause prompt action should be taken to rid the lilies of it. With lilies it is not good sense to wait and see if things get better.

PROPAGATION

There are a number of ways available for increasing lilies. The simplest but not the most prolific is by **Division**. Many species and most hybrids will naturally divide so that where there was one main stem last year there are two this. The gardener can easily break these apart in the autumn, replanting them immediately thereafter if possible. This ensures the bulbs do not become overcrowded and deteriorate. Although a method of increasing stock the practice of division and transplanting may be considered part of general cultivation.

Likewise many lilies will, initially by young leaves about the base of the plant, be seen to grow **Bulblets** on the stem below ground. Some cultivars are quite prodigious in providing increase by this means. Again it is an autumn task to reap this natural harvest. When the stem has withered, if the soil is loosened around the remaining coarse fibres, it may usually be detached from the mother bulb without other disturbance. Carefully the little bulbs may be prised off the old stem and their young tender roots withdrawn from the old tangled mass. If there are many from several bulbs the bulblets may be graded by size, the smallest being treated to pot culture or a sheltered nursery bed for a season. The larger, if required, may serve to broaden the planting or provide a new patch elsewhere. Depth of planting may be related to size; the smallest being covered by no more than an inch of friable humus-filled soil.

A few species, notably L. *tigrinum* (L. *lancifolium*) amongst the Asiatics and L. *sargentiae* for the trumpet lilies, sport small **Stem**

bulbils above ground. Fortunately this characteristic has been carried into numerous hybrid progeny and allows for propagation on a fairly large scale if the grower has a mind to it and the resources for growing on. All that is required is for the bulbils to be harvested usually in late summer and for them to be 'sown' as soon as possible thereafter in prepared nursery rows. Expecting that the baby bulbs will stay two seasons in the beds, the ground should be well prepared and the top tilth improved, as necessary, with the addition of peat or leaf soil and coarse sand if the basic loam is heavy. A site with partial shade should be chosen. The bulbils may be placed an inch apart (2.5cm) in rows 6 to 8 inches apart (15–20cm) covering the drills with about an inch of soil (2.5cm). Care should be taken to keep the beds as free of weeds as possible while the bulbils are dormant to alleviate the tiresome task in spring and summer when the young lily plants are easily damaged. If there are only a few bulbils then initially they can be grown in a pot.

The keen amateur, perhaps having paid a fairly high price for some special lilies, may wish to insure against possible losses as well as multiply his stock. Propagation by **Bulb scales** snapped off the base of the bulb is a relatively easy method of increase. It may be done at any suitable time but autumn is usually the easiest. Although a bulb may be completely denuded and the scales lined out in boxes in a 50/50 mixture of sand and peat, most people are content to break off a few of the outermost plump scales and place them with a sterile peat and grit mixture in a new clean plastic bag tightly tied and suitably labelled and placed in a warmish cupboard. After three weeks or so tiny bulbs are usually visible growing from the base of the scale. According to vigour in another two or three weeks the new bulblets will be ready for careful transfer to sterilised compost in pots. If the lilies are like L. *martagon*, having a winter dormancy, they may require a 3-month period in refrigeration before potting up, otherwise they will lie idle, possibly rotting off before springing into growth after the following winter.

Many lily enthusiasts like to grow lilies from **Seed**. This is the only way many of the species may be obtained, but few kinds of lilies are stocked by seed merchants. This is one of the many ways specialist societies help and encourage their members. Annually the RHS Lily Group issues an extensive list including species, hybrids and other Liliaceae. Contributors to the scheme come from many parts of the world as well as Britain. Lily societies in other countries act similarly. Through these voluntary agencies many more lilies are in cultivation than otherwise would be.

Generally lilies take longer to mature from seed, but many will produce a flower or two in the second year. Given sufficient warmth and light it is possible to obtain the lovely white trumpet flowers of L. formosanum in less than a year. To be fair, it is necessary to point out that many lilies are rather slow and take some years to reach flowering. However, they are likely to be either unobtainable or very expensive as good sized bulbs. To anyone who has the patience and is willing to learn a little skill it is a most rewarding pastime.

Unless large numbers are required seed is best sown in half pots or other suitable containers of a similar or greater depth. Adequate drainage should be allowed for and a suitable compost may be made from John Innes No. 1 compost with extra grit or coarse sand added to ensure an open mixture which will not clog later on. Sowing should be done thinly and evenly because the tiny bulbs are to stay in this compost until they are sufficiently large to handle carefully without fear of damage. Sprinkle some compost over them, giving a cover no more than 5–7mm deep. Using half-pots, when the seedlings have grown substantially, but not sufficiently to risk transferring individually the whole potful may be transferred to larger and deeper pots containing fresh and richer compost. After another season they will be ready to be lined out in a suitable place outdoors or, perhaps, some to their permanent positions.

There are two forms of germination: one where the seed germinates and make a little bulb underground but shows nothing above ground in the first season: the martagon lilies germinate in this way. In the other the seed germinates, usually in spring, and shortly sends a thin leaf-like appendage above ground somewhat like an onion seedling. The Asiatic hybrids are of this second kind as are the trumpet hybrids. The Orientals belong basically to the first with what is often called delayed germination. Many American lilies can act differently again so there are in fact a whole range of circumstances each varying slightly in degree. Readers may like to seek more information in Growing Lilies (see p.60), but if in doubt as to what to do with lily seed the best practice is to sow it immediately in pots, keeping them in a shaded protected site such as cold frame or under the bench of a cold greenhouse covered at first to minimise evaporation.

DISEASES, DISORDERS AND PESTS

As in all branches of gardening and horticulture there are problems to be tackled and lilies have their fair share in the pests and diseases that attack them. The case has been overstated at times and given the lilies a bad name. This is unfortunate because

'Eros', a scented, pink-flowered hybrid raised by Dr North (see p.48).

although lilies have some serious troubles like virus diseases, they seem to suffer no more than many other widely cultivated plants.

Diseases. The biggest nuisance is the fungus *Botrytis elliptica* which first shows following wet, close conditions in the spring. Attack usually starts on the leaves near the base which soon wither and die on the stem. In serious attacks all the foliage may be killed, the stem rot and the flower buds are ruined. The bulb is rarely killed, but is badly debilitated. Control is improved where there is a free circulation of air, but in any case early spraying is advisable, say, when the plants are at half height, with bordeaux mixture or other copper preparations. These have proved more effective than many recent fungicides. Repeat sprays adjusted to the weather conditions should be given even through the summer if necessary.

Another troublesome disease is **Basal rot** or *Fusarium oxysporum*, which as implied attacks the base of the bulb. Careful scrutiny should be given to all bulbs planted which should be into fresh ground where possible. Dead or affected scales should be removed and rotted portions cut out and burned. Remaining bulbs may then be sterilised in 2% formalin or dipped in benomyl.

'Pandora', a very early, orange-flowered hybrid of dwarf habit.

It is better to isolate doubtful bulbs in order not to contaminate the soil and this is best done by growing in pots for a season.

Other fungus diseases which affect the bulbs are *Rhizoctonia*, *Phytophthora* and *Penicillium* or blue mould. Good cultivation is the best preventive for these diseases. Good drainage, but never too dry conditions, allowing bulbs to be out of the ground for only the minimum period necessary means that bulbs and plants should never have to experience stressful conditions. Benomyl and other fungicides may often prove effective, but you should only resort to these chemicals when there is a serious problem.

Lilies suffer from a number of **virus diseases**. Some are killed rapidly when attacked while others are more tolerant and may survive, even performing satisfactorily if with less vigour. Although there are obvious symptoms such as mottled and curled foliage and broken flowers, there are others which go unnoticed and so it may be our pride and joy is harbouring a killer disease to another kind of lily. In these circumstances different kinds of lilies should be separated in the garden and kept apart from tulips. Separation by permanent subjects, such as conifers and shrubs, particularly evergreens, seems the most effective.

There is no cure for virus infection. Affected plants should be burnt. New stock may be raised from seed if available, as this does not carry the viruses into the new generation.

Disorders. From time to time the weather plays tricks with us, particularly frosts in spring, and lilies may grow up with distortions and buds made blind. It is possible to imagine many dire troubles, but next season they may not be apparent. Therefore before discarding any bulbs on to the funeral pyre it is best to be sure and this means waiting awhile, seeking advice, and not being too hasty.

Fasciation is another disorder which occurs fairly often in lilies. The flat stem which arises is really composed of two or more stems growing together. The cause may be a sudden change in growing conditions the previous season or possibly a flourishing bulb becoming too dry in autumn to complete its division into two bulbs. Although many more flowers are produced the overall effect is usually aesthetically poor. The lily rights itself the next season.

Petal doubling occurs now and again. This is not excessive; an odd flower may have nine petals. Reversion to normal the following year suggests a minor curiosity, not a cause to worry.

Should the **foliage colour change** from a uniform green to a purplish brown, possibly flecked, then there is trouble below ground. Investigation will most likely show no basal root growth or rotting roots and a spent and rotting bulb. Unless the bulb through previous bad storage has not initiated roots the cause is likely to be poor soil drainage. If not too far gone the bulb should be cleaned up for replanting elsewhere where the drainage is good or scaled to produce new bulblets.

Should the **leaves appear yellowish** and chlorotic and the gardener knows his soil to be chalky, limey, and so definitely alkaline, the lily is most likely one of the acid lovers. Some lilies are definitely not lime tolerant and if the gardener wants to grow them, the pH of the soil must be reduced. This may be done in the longer term by adding acid humus, best in the form of moss peat, sulphur and sulphate of ammonia. However this action will not get quickly to the root of the problem so spraying with a chelated iron compound may be the initial immediate answer.

Pests. Although lilies may be subject to a large number of pests the gardener will usually only be troubled seriously by a few. These are also serious pests of other garden plants and so are not specific to lilies.

Many **Aphids**, commonly called greenflies, attack lilies. They feed on the young tissues and seriously distort growth, flower buds and generally weaken the plant. If this was not enough, they are the commonest vectors in transferring virus diseases from plant to plant. For this reason alone lily growers must always ensure that aphids are kept down to the minimum by regular spraying with an insecticide, such as malathion or a systemic, such as dimethoate or heptenophos. A careful watch should be made for the first signs of aphids in the garden and whether apparent on lilies or not the first spray should then be given.

Next in importance are usually **Slugs**. The species both above and below ground attack lilies ravenously. War must be waged on them unmercifully. Slug pellets of metaldehyde or methiocarb give a very good control for the species above ground. The latter seem to be effective for a longer period, but it may be wise to use the two kinds alternately to stem any build up of resistance to these baits. If keeled slugs are in the soil below ground it would be better not to use the area for lilies, but to drench it with liquid metaldehyde. Frequent cultivation is very beneficial, as is the marked 'planting' of pieces of potato for bait (cheaper than lilies!) to be subsequently dug up holding the catch. The most vulnerable time for the lilies is early spring when there is the combination of moisture and warmth. A look out should always be kept for the clusters of whitish round eggs just below ground level which are easily destroyed.

Lily beetle appears to have become a more serious pest in southern England in recent years. A careful watch should be kept from late March onwards in order to take prompt action should it be necessary. The mature bright red beetle, with black legs and head, overwinters in the soil and possible frequents that of a lighter sandy nature. Both beetle and larvae (somewhat like birds' droppings) eat the lily foliage voraciously but will also attack stems and flowers. The beetles can be collected by picking them off the plants but they and their larvae are easily controlled by many well known insecticide sprays, such as permethrin, HcH or fenitrothion.

If **Wireworms, Leatherjackets** or **Millipedes** are in the soil they are likely to attack lily bulbs. As a preventive measure one of the proprietary soil pest killers such as diazinon, phoxim or bromophos, should be sprinkled closely around when planting. When lifting bulbs a careful watch should be kept for any particular damage in order to ascertain the cause.

Birds are sometimes seen to do damage. The most commonly noticed is the pecking of the bases of unopened flower buds for the nectar within. Although a nuisance when it occurs this is hardly a great problem and the lily grower gets many advantages from the birds. Various **Rodents** can be troublesome at times feeding on the bulbs in winter, but it is not commonplace. Such factors as extreme weather conditions, lack of normal food supply and population pressures play their part. Larger animals, like

Rabbits and even **Deer** may take to eating lilies if the garden is exposed to such pests and it may be necessary to surround clumps of lilies with wire netting in order to protect them.

This hybrid has outward-facing orange flowers spotted with black.

Lilium 'Oliver Wyatt' (see p.49).

What lilies to grow

Until the 1940s most of the lilies grown were the species. During the forty years before that the enthusiasts had tried hard to produce good hybrids and had in fact done much of the basic work, but it was not until after the second World War with the efforts of Jan de Graaff at the Oregon Bulb Farms that the hybrids began to steal the thunder. Now there is a vast range of hybrids and for most garden purposes they are in many ways superior and less fastidious than the species. Even so some of the species have not been superseded and so seriously deserve treatment here.

SPECIES

The cottage garden lily *par excellence*, the white lily, the symbol of the Madonna, *L. candidum* (see pp11 & 33), is possibly the commonest lily grown in the southern half of Britain. Although now there are different fertile kinds grown in some gardens, the one usually seen is an infertile clone that has been in cultivation for hundreds of years. It is easily grown in a sunny site preferably in a neutral or alkaline soil with the bulbs planted in August only just below the surface. Unfortunately it is susceptible to botrytis and also carries virus disease to which it is tolerant so should be grown away from other lilies.

In the northern half of Britain the orange lily, *L. bulbiferum croceum*, is quite commonly seen flourishing in gardens large and small. Quite distinct not only by colour from the Madonna lily, but by its upright crocus-like flowers, it is easy to establish. Perhaps it is superseded by various hybrids, but few give so much for so little attention.

Two lilies are naturalised in Britain. They are the Pyrenean lily, *L. pyrenaicum* (see p.51), and the whorled-leaved martagon lily, *L. martagon* (see p.13). Both have turkscap flowers, the first usually yellow, sometimes red, but always spotted, and the latter a shade of mauvy pink, often purple or spotless white. They are both excellent in the wild garden but need not be confined there. The Pyrenean lily is fine for being one of the earliest to flower sometimes in late May and the martagon lily in its better coloured forms or the pure white has a stately charm and beauty in the border otherwise unmatched.

Another species which has settled itself seemingly with

43

Golden Splendour, showing the parts of the flower (see p.8).

A clump of pastel hybrids at RHS Garden, Wisley.

permanence in a number of gardens across the country is the Caucasian lily, L. *szovitsianum* (see p.15). It has a handsome yellow flower not so tightly recurved as a turkscap and tending to look at you rather than hang its head. It is a pity that it is slow to mature and difficult to obtain.

Quite different in most respects is the diminutive L. *formosanum pricei* from Taiwan. It is a perfect trumpet lily, small only in stature and easily raised from seed to flower the following season. It fits neatly in the rock garden or the front of the border.

This is no place to mention all the species which number about one hundred, but it seems wrong not to recall L. *regale* (see cover) that Ernest Wilson found tucked away in a distant valley in western China early this century. He freed it from the encircling mountains and gave to gardeners a stalwart but most beautiful white and golden-throated trumpet lily all could cultivate.

HYBRIDS

The first group to discuss contains the Asiatic hybrids. They are by far the most numerous, perhaps the most important, and across the world the most widely grown. Very few people who grow lilies do not have one or more of these. The group is easily divided into three sections: those that have upright flowers, those that are outward-facing and the third kind where the flowers are pendent. Until comparatively recently the colour range was from yellow through orange to red and the dark shades of orange-red. Today white and pinks are easily obtained and there is better scope in the red spectrum.

Besides many with the natural spotting there are now well known cultivars completely spotless, giving a vividness of colour unashamedly brilliant. If this is too much for some of us then more recently still have come the 'brushmark' lilies so adequately describing this interesting petal marking. There is more yet to be seen with two and three toned and colour-edged flowers. Stamina has fortunately been no great problem with Asiatic hybrids, while stature has been seen to be suitably variable with the parents showing greatly differing height characteristics. So it is that there are cultivars ranging from a foot to 6 feet in height (30cm–2m) and the tallest rarely require staking except in exposed situations.

Choosing from such a broad range for a wide variety of situations is no enviable task, but it is made more difficult (or easier?) by lack of availability. Fortunately after a bleak period of many years there now seems to be more opportunity for buying lily bulbs in Britain. Basically, there are two main sources of supply, the supermarket and garden centres and the smaller nursery-men/bulb specialists. The larger bulb merchant fits awkwardly into the former group as he tends to supply imported bulbs similar to those packeted for retail trade.

The commonest and most famous upright flowering lily is the nasturtium-red 'Enchantment' (see p.55). Not really as good as it was made out to be, but far better well grown in the garden than when seen as offered in the flower trade throughout twelve months of the year. In other shades of red are 'Scarlet Emperor', 'Pirate' and 'Firecracker'. For yellow there are the spotless

'Marilyn Monroe' has golden-yellow flowers (see p.48).

'Connecticut King' (see p.9), 'Marilyn Monroe' (see p.47) and 'Phoebus'. White, or more precisely palest cream, are 'Mont Blanc' and 'Sterling Star'. Those to be recommended with outward-facing flowers are 'Minos' and 'Orestes', red and salmon-orange respectively, the yellow 'Connecticut Maid', the pink 'Hawaiian Punch' and blood-red 'Garnet Light'.

The pendent-flowered types have tended more recently to be dominated at least in this country by the hybrids raised by Dr North using *L. lankongense* in their parentage. Generally the flowers are more turkscap in form than those outward or upright facing. 'Theseus' (see p.62), 'Ariadne' (see p.59), 'Eros' (see p.37) and 'Iona' (see p.2) are all from the North stable and vary in colour from dark crimson to a pale pink-coral. For yellow shades we may go to other raisers to mention 'Hornback's Gold' and 'Beckwith Tiger'. In orange-red there is the spotless 'Connecticut Yankee' and 'Orange Wattle'.

The second group is referred to as the Martagon hybrids and concerns all those five or so species which are closely related and form a unique group. *Lilium martagon* itself (see pp.13 & 26) in one of its varieties or forms is usually one of the parents and initially *L. hansonii* was the other. Whereas *L. martagon* covers a vast range across Europe and through much of Siberia, *L. hansonii*, fortunately for hybridisers orange-yellow in colour, inhabits only Ullang-Do, and island to the east of South Korea. This species grows happily in our gardens as do the hybrid progeny. The trouble though in recommending these lilies is their lack of availability. They take longer to mature as commercial bulbs and so are spurned by bulb producers. Perhaps if the demand was larger and more certain the situation would change. Names used for the hybrids include 'Marhan', × *dalhansonii*, Paisley Hybrids, Backhouse Hybrids and 'Ellen Willmott'. In recent years some keen amateurs have been making new crosses including *L. tsingtauense* and *L. medeoloides* within the hybrid framework and some interesting developments are taking place.

The third group is the smallest of the hardy lilies and concerns the few hybrids made with *L. chalcedonicum*, the lovely red turkscap lily from Greece, and the well-known Madonna lily. It might not have been worth mentioning at all, but there are two reasons so to do. Firstly, the original lily hybrid produced was indeed a cross between this white trumpet-type lily, *L. candidum* and *L. chalcedonicum* of turkscap form. It is called *L.* × *testaceum* and is still much in existence today after nearly two centuries. It is a beautiful lovely pale nankeen yellow. It may be found in many different kinds of gardens from the largest to the most lowly, but nevertheless is much sought after. The second reason is that a few enthusiasts are trying to produce this cross again and are also trying to emulate Oliver Wyatt's hybrids that he produced at the end of the last war using L. x *testaceum* as one of the parents. It is hoped they meet with success.

Species native to North America are the parents of hybrids making the fourth group. The lovely but somewhat capricious species from the eastern states have played virtually no role in the hybrids to date, so they are based on the western or Pacific Coast species. They are a tall stately group, the flowers being mainly of the turkscap kind but often less tightly recurved and placed on elegant curving pedicels; the leaves are carried in whorls. These hybrids enjoy light woodland and bring new colour to spring-flowering shrub gardens in July but will stand unabashed in the sunlit border if so desired. The Bellingham Hybrids are the most famous in this group and of this number 'Shuksan' is perhaps the best of all. Oliver Wyatt, late Chairman of the Lily Committee and Treasurer of the RHS, gave his name to one of the most beautiful yellow lilies showing a strong influence of L. *parryi* (see p.42). Another in this class is 'Coachella'. Del Norte Hybrids were possibly the first pink kinds in this class, but have now been superseded by 'Lake Tahoe' (see p.58) and 'Lake Tulare' produced here. The best red tones and missing the garish orange shades, come in the Bullwood Hybrids with selections like 'Cherrywood' (see p.50). These western American Hybrids grow well in Britain and are proving so on the continent. A few are trying them again in USA where strangely they have always been found difficult. They seem to have a reasonable lime tolerance.

Another very small group are the hybrids between the less hardy L.*longiflorum*, and L. *formosanum* and L. *philippinense*. Unless greenhouse culture can be given these are unlikely to be successful. Even so the general reaction of those that know is that many of the varieties of L. *longiflorum* are superior to the hybrid strains.

Following from the last paragraph the real trumpet lilies for garden decoration, combined with the Aurelian Hybrids, come into this sixth group. Although in effect they took many years to produce, these highly coloured flowers seemed to explode as out of a jack-in-the-box in front of the gardening public a few years after the last War. Their development continued by selection for a while,but has not progressed much further in the last thirty years. This, however, need not trouble the gardener. Because of the inclusion of L. *henryi* (see p.14), having recurved petals, within their ranks, these lilies vary greatly in their size and shape. Four types are recognised: the formal trumpet, bowl-shaped pendent and the flat star-shaped. Those available today include African

Above: *L. bulbiferum typicum*
Below: 'Cherrywood', one of the Bullwood Hybrids (see p. 49).
Opposite: *L. pyrenaicum* naturalised in Aberdeenshire (see p. 43).

Queen, Golden Sunburst and Golden Splendor (see p.44). A cooler shade is provided by Green Magic and for those who like their beetroots on tall lily stems, Pink Perfection. Heart's Desire has a more open bowl of white with golden centre. All these may be produced from seed strains without too much difficulty so for those with a little patience and not too deep a pocket a whole wealth of lovely lilies may be theirs.

Left until the last are the most flamboyant, the largest and yet often the most beautiful flowers that come with the Oriental hybrids. Usually they are later flowering, coming into bloom in August or even September. They are based on L. × parkmannii a cross between L. auratum the largest of all lily flowers (see p.16) and L. speciosum so often seen in florists' windows. Both of these come from Japan as do other species that have been used in some of the more recent hybrids. No orange is apparent in the flowers, only a yellow is seen at times in the centre or as rays in the petals. The basic colours are pink and red on white. Shape gives us three forms which may be described as bowl-shaped, flat and recurved When fully grown they are tall stately plants carrying many large flowers. In such a condition they demand staking. They are not lime tolerant so need an acid soil and look best in light shade. They are susceptible to virus diseases and should be kept apart from other lilies which may be tolerant but carrying the disease. These lilies may be expected to be the dearest especially for novelties. The palest or whitest come in the Imperial Silver Strain. Where the yellow rays are prominent they are called Imperial Gold. If the yellow is substituted by red rays then they are Redband Hybrids. When the colour spreads gorgeously across the petals they are named Imperial Pink or Imperial Crimson and when the petals are recurved Jamboree strain. All these names refer to hybrids produced originally by Jan de Graaff at the Oregon Bulb Farms, but many others have been produced particularly in New Zealand and Australia, where the Oriental hybrids are grown to perfection.

Before completing this condensed survey of lily cultivars there is room to mention one more. It was said that L. henryi, not a trumpet lily, had been used to modify the trumpet flower in the many hybrids often called Aurelians. This species has also been crossed with L. speciosum to which in flower, except in colour, it looks so similar. The hybrid was named 'Black Beauty'. Not black by any means but certainly a beauty, it is in simple terms like a very dark coloured L. speciosum. Although sterile itself that hurdle has been jumped by using a tetraploid form. As these lilies are metaphorically on the frontiers of their clan they are exciting developments giving us a tantalising glimpse of lilies of the future.

Exhibiting lilies

The pronounced competitive spirit which exists among enthusiastic cultivators of such as the narcissus, the dianthus and the rose, does not show itself with the lily. The London shows have their serried ranks for other genera but despite some effort in recent years it has not really happened for lilies. Generally the British lily grower has remained unmoved. It is certainly not the case in other countries where lilies are grown to any marked extent, because, for instance, in North America and in the Antipodes, distinct lily shows are organised and the basis of thes shows are competitive classes.

However, the British lily grower may still wish, or be inveigled, into showing his best blooms. The London competition still exists, the co-operative display welcomes amateur gardeners to provide material and throughout the country many local horticultural societies provide a class for a vase of lilies. Here, if nowhere else, is the opportunity to win a cup for the best exhibit in the show.

Aside from the elation of winning there are with lilies the usual number of pitfalls in exhibiting. No lily year is said to be a good one and so the grower must watch his specimens closely in the days of June and early July. Season and weather will play its part and judgement of when flowers will open is, surprisingly for the time of the year, not always easy. So what will be available on the day and how to organise for that is a matter of good judgement tempered by past experience.

When cutting has to begin suitable receptacles with water should be already available. It might be the cool of evening, but if it has been hot, the stems will be improved by a good draught of water. For some period of hours it is assumed they will be without any. Careful handling is essential and no stress must be placed on the stems or pedicels that will distort the inflorescence. If the anthers and their pollen are likely to smudge the petals they should be encapsuled in thin aluminium foil. In no case should they be removed, as the lilies are not complete without them.

Good packing comes only with experience, so without the latter we must try our best. There must be firmness without rigidity. Conventional boxes with plenty of tissue paper are satisfactory for some specimens, but prize stems are often generously proportioned and need containers of greater depth. If the stems are to be

Opposite: A seedling of 'Wattle Bird', a hybrid raised in Australia.
Above, top: A modern unspotted Connecticut hybrid.
Above: 'Enchantment', often seen as a cut flower in florists shops.

55

supported on a bridge, so to speak, then they should be given the necessary strength by thin bamboo sticks tied neatly along their length. If it is possible the best way to carry the flowers is vertically such as in a suitably tall van. With the aid of some carpentry, rows of vases with water and individual stems can be driven hundreds of miles without stress to flower or worry to exhibitor.

No time should be lost at the show site in getting the lilies into their vases and supported, if necessary, for a freshening up spell. Any damaged flowers should be cut off cleanly at the base of the pedicel. Any pollen or other marks should be carefully cleaned off. Remember pollen is sticky and adheres rather tenaciously. If it is a competition make sure you know the rules and schedule well and are interpreting them correctly. Many an otherwise good exhibit is unfortunately placed NAS (*not according to schedule*) rather than amongst the winners. When staging is completed check your entries with their cards thoroughly. After that a recheck is wise as neither the show secretary nor his stewards are there to get you out of trouble.

Creating new lilies

The wealth of seed made available by lily enthusiasts for distribution seems to grow annually. There are sterile clones and sterile lines of development, but even so there still appear great opportunities for producing new and better hybrid lilies. The actual task is not difficult for anybody willing to take a little trouble.

The sexual parts of a lily are perfectly obvious to anybody. Most lilies produce pollen in plenty on large anthers and the stigma is obvious and sticky just waiting for the gardener to lend a hand. Sometimes insects or rough weather will do the job more readily, so precautions should be taken against these. All that is then required is a reasonable summer and fine autumn to obtain plump seeds. Again these are easily procured and as soon as they are ripe, picked, cleaned of chaff, etc, ready for sowing.

Pollen dabbing, therefore, is easy, but controlled pollination with a premeditated plan is generally more worthwhile. With a plan records should be kept and this will provide not only the facts in time to come, but an understanding of the possibilities and the problems.

In Britain our summers are so variable that seed is not so easily produced of, say, the Oriental hybrids, as it is in some other countries. These are generally late flowering and the seed takes time to mature. Certain other crosses will not prove easy here as more heat seems necessary to make certain of viable seed. Outlandish crosses, ie, those with parents falling in different groups, should not be attempted, at least, until the hybridiser knows more about the subject. The recommendation would be to start with something simple, possibly amongst the Asiatic group, in order to achieve a worthwhile result, while keeping an eye on the main goal.

Further Reading

Having whetted the appetite for the engaging pastime of growing lilies it is essential to append a list of worthwhile books which go more deeply into the many aspects of cultivating and studying lilies. Lily books, unlike some subjects in gardening, are not published very frequently, so do not let an early date of publication put you off. There are many words of wisdom covered by

Above: 'Lake Tahoe', raised in England from American species.
Opposite, top: 'Pink Glory', seen here in the Savill Gardens, Windsor.
Opposite: 'Ariadne', a hybrid raised by Dr North (see p. 48).

enough dust in which we might otherwise grow a few lilies. If a book is out of print or otherwise not obtainable go to the library and order it. It may take time but likely as not the most difficult book to find will duly turn up.

Elwes, H. J. (1877–80) *A Monograph of the Genus Lilium*. This is a magnificent giant tome and extremely valuable. Probably only available in specialist libraries. Between 1933 and 1940 A. Grove and A. D. Cotton produced seven parts of *A Supplement to Elwes' Monograph of the Genus Lilium*. This also is large and rare. W. B. Turrill (1960–2) produced parts 8 and 9 of the Supplement.

Evans, A. (1974) *The Peat Garden and its Plants*. Dent. London. Twenty two pages are devoted to Lily species and other *Liliaceae* suitable for the enviroment described.

Feldmaier, C. (1970) *Die Neuen Lilien*. Ulmer, Stuttgart. An English translation was subsequently published by Batsford (1970). Since then a new revised edition in collaboration with Judith McRae has been published (1982) and an edition in English is awaited in the USA.

Fox, Derek. (1985) *Growing Lilies*. Croom Helm, London. This is the latest addition to the literature endeavouring to treat both the species and hybrids in sufficient detail to satisfy the enthusiast and keen gardener.

Graaff, Jan de & Hyams, Edward. (1967) *Lilies*. London. Tells the story of the lilies from the famous Oregon Bulb Farms.

Jekyll, Gertrude. (1901) *Lilies for English Gardens*. Country Life, London. Not a great book on lilies despite the famous author. There have been at least two reprints in recent years.

Leeburn, M. E. (1955) *Lilies and their Cultivation*. London. A Foyles handbook.

Marshall, W. E. (1929) *Consider the Lilies* and supplement (1930), New York. An interesting piece of American advertising of the time.

Maxwell, Alice C. (1953) *Lilies in their Homes*. Collins, London. Describes the lilies both in their native haunts and for the gardener at home.

North American Lily Society has since 1948 produced an excellent series of Yearbooks and quarterly bulletins containing a wealth of information provided by contributors from the various continents as well as North America.

Parkinson, J. (1629) *Paradisi in Sole Paradisus terrestris*. London. Besides the beautiful title this is the best seventeenth century work on lilies and their culture.

Royal Horticultural Society has over the years provided a wealth of information on lilies in its *Journal* (now *The Garden*) and the *Lily Year Books* Nos 1 to 34 (1932–71). Since 1972 similar softbacks have been produced by the Lily Committee and Lily Group culminating in *Lilies and Related Plants 1984/85*.

Stern, F. C. (1960) *A Chalk Garden*, rev. 1974. Faber, London. Sir Frederick was the first and for many years Chairman of the Lily Committee.

Stoker, F. (1943) *A Book of lilies*. Penguin, London and New York. This is a little King Penguin with small but lovely coloured plates.

Synge, P. M. (1961) *Collins' Guide to Bulbs*. Collins, London. Devotes 38 pages to detailing both species and hybrids.

Synge, P. M. (1980) *Lilies*. Batsford, London. Is the most sumptuous recent work with many fine coloured plates.

Wallace, A. (1879) *Notes on Lilies and their Culture*. 2nd edition, Colchester. Is a fascinating and complex nineteenth century guide to lily growing.

Wilson, E. H. (1925) *The Lilies of Eastern Asia, a Monograph* has the words of both the botanist and the intrepid explorer.

Woodcock, H. B. D. & Stearn, W. T. (1950) *Lilies of the World, Their Cultivation and Classification*, Country Life, London. Has become the authoritative post–war guide to everything about lilies.

THE LILY GROUP

The Royal Horticultural Society has had a Lily Committee for over fifty years and one of the major tasks of the Committee is to run the Lily Group. In doing so the Committee organises exhibitions

Above 'Theseus', a very vigorous, scented, *lankongense* hybrid
(see p.48).
Opposite: 'Achilles', a late-flowering hybrid with upright-facing flowers.

of Lilies and *Liliaceae* at the RHS Halls in London, provides lectures, discussions and periodic conferences, publishes a regular newsletter and currently a biennial year book, arranges outings to gardens and similar institutions, runs a worldwide seed distribution scheme and holds an annual bulb auction. In these and other ways, including co-operation with other similar societies, it does all in its power to promote the cultivation and understanding of lilies and related genera. Membership is available for the price of a modest subscription and all those interested are requested to write to the secretary, Mrs Ann Dadd, 21 Embrook Road, Wokingham, Berkshire, RG11 1HF.